For Singles

IN PREPARATION

Damilola, The Lord will send His best to you. IJN Akanle 7/22/17

Toyin Akanle

FOREWORDED BY PASTOR TOLA ODUTOLA

Singles In Preparation

Copyright © 2017

Collustrations Media LLC
1813 Long Leaf Way
Servern MD 21144
www.collustrations.com
Email: project@collustrations.com

Cover design and content page design
by Collustration Media, LLC
Published in Servern, Maryland
by Collustrations Media, LLC

Contributor
Pastor Dele Akanle

Edited by
Pastor Shaunna Jackson Agboju

Co-edited by
Dr. Odunayo Obisesan

TABLE OF
CONTENT

Acknowledgements

I really want to thank the Lord Almighty, for leading me to write "Singles In Preparation" I am also grateful for the strength and courage He gave me not to give up even when I felt like it. Unto Him immortal, invincible, all knowing be all thanks and praise.

To my darling husband of decades; Darl, Pastor Oladele Akanle, your immeasurable contributions to this work and your support of the same is priceless. Thank you so much for being the love of my life, my pastor, my mentor, my prayer partner and much more. Thanks for always believing in me.

Demi, Temi and Nimi, my greatest miracles from God after my Salvation and my husband, you guys are the best. Thanks for your understanding, encouragement, suggestion and support. I am grateful to God for the wonderful children you are.

I want to thank Pastor Tola Odutola; a mentor, a good listener, with wealth of godly counsels. You constantly encourage us to believe in ourselves and be the best we can. Thank you for taking time to read and forward this book.

A big thanks to Mr. George Thesis, for granting me the permission to use his very insightful article, "Parental Permission To Marry" in this work. I appreciate you.

My wonderful Editor, Pastor Shaunna Jackson Agboju for your wonderful editing of this work, my printer Collustration, you are awesome. My wonderful sister in the lord, Alison Ephraim who saw the gift in me and encouraged me to go for it. My big sister Dr. Odunayo Obisesan who at some point co-edited this work and gave me the push to continue.

I also acknowledge every single male and female whose questions are used in this book, thanks for your open mindedness.

I truly acknowledge the immense support and encouragement of everyone who made this book possible, thanks.

Dedication

This book is dedicated to the originator of godly marriage; the Almighty God Himself, who instituting such a wonderful medium of love, companionship, sharing and joy.

Forward

Today, the institution of marriage is under a great attack both from state and many other angles. However, the Scripture cannot be broken as Bible tells us that marriage is "...*honorable among all and the bed undefiled*..." Hebrews 13:4a.

In this book, Pastor (Mrs.) Toyin Akanle has highlighted to us, the many steps to a successful relationship. I believe without a doubt that if we follow these steps, our marriages and relationships will be filled with testimonies.

I therefore recommend this book for all singles and married couples and to be used as a teaching tool for many seeking testimony-filled marriages and relationships.

Happy reading.

Pastor Tola Odutola

Introduction

For any endeavor to succeed in life there must be some planning and calculated preparations. Often, when things are done without adequate planning and preparation, the result of such endeavor will likely be chaotic and ultimate failure. The Scriptures has this to say about planning and preparation;

> *"If one of you wanted to build a tower, wouldn't you first sit down and calculate the cost, to determine whether you have enough money to complete it? Otherwise, when you have laid the foundation but couldn't finish the tower, all who see it will begin to belittle you. They will say, 'Here's the person who began construction and couldn't complete it!"*
> Luke 14:28-30 (Common English Bible).

This is true about the issue of marriage. Like every other venture, marriage is a lifetime venture and it also has its cost and rewards. Planning and preparation is therefore highly necessary. Single folks looking forward to marriage must be well prepared for this lifetime journey. It is better to know and be well prepared for what a person is embarking upon than to regret later.

Marriage is a holy institution initiated by God. However, marriage has been defined and redefined in so many ways such that it has lost its intended scriptural value. There is a lot of confusion, misgivings and misconceptions about marriage as we know it.

Most times, singles carry this confusion, misconception and misgivings into marriage and the prevalent result is widespread frustration which ultimately leads to high rate of separation and divorce in our societies. Even the Church is not spared this scourge.

One thing is clear though, God's stance, plan, and purpose for marriage is well established and has not changed. It is to foster unity, happiness and procreation.

Based on these two factors, the burden for *Singles In Preparation* was born. I strongly feel that It is very important therefore, to "look before you leap," when it comes to marriage, the launching pad been the word of God. It may be true that love is blind, but the reality is that one needs to *"keep one's eyes peeled and enlightened by the word of God"* when trying to go into a marriage. There are certain things to look out for, look at, and even enquire about.

It is better to find out certain things before saying "I do" than to be shocked and surprised afterward. If a partner finds out some negative things about his or her intending before marriage, he or she will be able to determine if it's worth embarking upon or not. There need to be a decision if he or she want to overlook the negative things, live with them, quit or just ignore them outright and move ahead with the union.

However, once marriage takes place, it is not that easy to leave the union. Scriptures tells us God hates divorce and every single person preparing for marriage must avoid it. Those who have unfortunately experienced separation and divorce did so with scars to remember. It's still preferable to wait than to regret later!

Singles in Preparation, is therefore based largely on offering godly counsel and answers to the common questions asked by Christian singles who have their eyes and hearts on marriage.

The Bible clearly says that where there are no counsels the people perish, It is my pleasure to be of tremendous help to all categories of singles out there who desire to have a memorable and happy marriage. I will like to point out that this has been possible with the help of God, He still has interest in marriages. It was His original idea in the first place. It's therefore in order to go back to God and seek strength and resolve to embark on this phenomenal lifetime venture. I still believe in a happy marriage. I believe that as singles, male and female alike, read this book, they will be exposed to materials that will get them ready and prepared for a glorious journey. Enjoy!

#1

"A well-suited **partner** does not mean A **perfectly** flawlessly **partner.**"

TOYIN AKANLE

How Do I Know God's Choice?
Of A Life Partner For Me ?

Perhaps this is the most common and basic question singles asks, and I think is fundamental and natural. Let's consider prevailing factors that influences singles in deciding this is Mr. Right and Miss Perfect.

For some it's love and what they have in common. To others, they just feel it's time to tie the knots because it seems right or they are of age. Some others are compelled by pressure from family, colleagues and even professional demands. In some cases, it could be through an intermediary like a Pastor or a spiritual figure, a relative, dating agency or an associate.

These factors are not bad in a sense because there are notable marriages that were initiated through these processes. Nevertheless, I would rather look at this all-important question by reframing the question to; *"Who and what would God want for me regarding a life partner?"*

It's best to answer the question from the Scriptures.

Originally, we are made to understand that what God desired for Adam was a "helpmeet", and for Eve, someone to love her and to take care of her. So, regarding the choice of a life partner, God's parameters are the best measure of knowing God's choice for you.

What I mean is using and considering biblical standards and parameters when deciding. For example, the scriptures clearly instructed Christians not to be unequally yoked with an unbeliever;

> *"Don't become partners with those who reject God.*
> *How can you make a partnership out of right and wrong?*
> *That's not partnership; that's war. Is light best friends with*
> *dark?*

(2 Corinthians 6:14). (The Message Bible).

No matter how sweet or agreeable an individual you have met and have an interest in is, as a Christian, a decent and safe litmus test in determining your marriage partner is whether the fellow has a genuine and sincere relationship with Christ.

Someone might point out that even sincere Christian marriages can be rocky at times too. As true as this argument may sound, the fact remains that, by far more Christian marriages withstand the assault on marriages than non-Christian marriages.

According to a Christianity Today's report posted on February 13 2012, the Evangelical Alliance's latest research found out that *"Christians are happier in their marriages and more likely to stay together than non-Christians"* A marriage relationship to a non-Christian is a no-go area for a true child of God. Your values, outlook to life, beliefs and desires are bound to be different and that right there is a prerequisite for disaster in marriage. You don't want to be added to statistics!

The safest way to get God to help you in deciding for your life partner is to deliberately allow the scriptures to be your guiding standard. Here prayer would prove to be a powerful tool. It will surprise you what you will learn and come to know when you make prayer a strong part of your deciding process. I am not suggesting the "fleece" type of prayer where you ask God to make the lady smile at you, or make the man wear a certain color of pant as a confirmation; but asking God for His help in deciding and looking toward your inner conviction, especially through the discerning of deep things will be in order. Prayer support from your Parents, Pastor or a reliable spiritual mentor will also be helpful.

However, beware of jumping around with prayer requests and looking for pastors to pray for you, else you will fall for matchmaking. Trust the servant of God that God has put you under his/her leadership as they pray and seek God's face with you.

Make it a point of duty to pray constantly about knowing God's choice for you in marriage. When you pray to God about a life

partner, He will certainly direct your hearts if you allow Him to guide you completely and you would be able to avoid mistakes. You therefore need to establish an active relationship with God if you have not already done so.

Being intimate with God always is very important, but I recommend you enhance your intimacy with God when you begin to sense the desire to settle down for matrimony. When you have built a strong relationship with the Almighty God, you will develop sensitivity to how God speaks or passes information to you. This is because people have different experiences with God and He can choose to relate with any person as He deem fit.

Permit me to use my case as an example. Even though I had been praying before I decided on my husband, and had absolute confirmation that he is God's choice for me. I recollect growing cold feet with my decision because in my culture there is the "popular" belief that if a man has many sisters, the bride would be oppressed, suppressed and terrorized. Of course, there is no basis for this unfounded belief. But as I grew cold feet, I spent more time praying and kept asking God for direction in decision making. My guiding text was Luke.5:5b;

"...but because you say so, I'll drop the nets."

■ 5 |

This became my inner witness and the more I meditated on this bible text the more I had the assurance that this was God speaking to me. God had in time past guided me this way and I had every reason to believe this was God's leading. Twenty-four years after, my marriage is still waxing strong in the Lord. No regrets!

I would also like to mention that you need to put your trust in God to lead you to the right person. His promise is to give His children the best of all things, even a life partner. He will surely guide you to choose the right partner well-suited for you. But be aware that a well-suited partner does not mean the partner will be flawlessly perfect. You can be sure God will bring someone who will grow into you and grow with you. Putting your trust in God helps you eliminate the risk of choosing the wrong person, knowing well that God has good plans for you (Jer.29:11).

What we (my husband and I) generally counsel singles, is to look for a person that has the fear and reverence for the things and ways of God. This is key in knowing a person's character. It is the foundation of every good marriage relationship. The fear of God controls every other thing. You need someone who will listen and adhere to God's views, perspective, and demands in all circumstances. If you find such an individual, hey, go ahead and thrust yourself into God's hands, you are safe with Him.

There must also be some level of chemistry between you and your intended, if you have found one or you are interested in someone. I always emphasize affection when I counsel either in a pre-marital session or in a marriage seminar. Though there are folks who have gotten married through long distance relationship, it is always best to give affection a place in the relationship. I am not saying marriages contracted and maintained via long distance are bad, but healthy affection develops more through physical presence.

There is need to see who you will be getting into this union with, seeing each other physically affords you the opportunity to see things for yourself. As you seek God's guidance, you should try to find out if you even have any connection to him or her. In Genesis 2:23, Adam's face must have brightened up when he saw Eve. That must have been the chemistry that made the lonely man announce,

> "...This is now bone of my bones, and flesh of my flesh: she shall be called Woman, because she was taken out of Man...".

There was an immediate connection between them, call it love at first sight, if you like. The fact that Adam knows that God gave him the best was enough for him. He even named her based on his feelings for her. Don't downplay affection in your choice of a life partner. I believe God put affection in place in humans to foster and fuel relationship. By the way, in marriage, the test of your trust for your partner and your partner's loyalty will be based on affection for each other. Lack of sincere affection for each other is one of the reasons that make divorce a welcoming idea at the slightest mistake or misstep in a marriage relationship. The constituents of love, friendship in any relationship is affection.

And of course, you must love the person and know you are loved in return. Talking about love, the love Christians ought to have towards their partner should be the Agape love – love at its ultimate; a self-sacrificing love. Often, when Christians refer to the agape love, they refer to the one they demonstrate toward fellow believers and others but not within the marriage setting. The kind of love we know as *'Phileo'* love; a brotherly love. You need agape love in the marriage setting as much as you require it in any other part of your life. Agape love overlooks and overrules all errors and mistakes and misbehaviors (1 Corinthians 13:6).

I must agree, it can be a case of *"easier said than done,"* but if from the onset, you base your choice on God's precepts, it will be easier to practice.

Everyone may find your partner boring and an irritant, but you won't notice it if the affection is naturally strong. Every other person you know might not also want you with him or her, but you know that is who you want to be with for the rest of your life. He may be clumsy, she may be untidy, but somehow you are drawn to him and her; that is affection. This is what draws God to us despite our numerous shortcomings, and yet we are still His priced bride and beloved people.

You must be ready to live with the person's shortcomings and all that makes him imperfect. It is not your similarities that will make the marriage, but what noticeable and acceptable differences you are ready to live with. Expect your spouse's imperfections to show forth right from the moment you both say *"I do,"*. Then be ready to forgive, because with time you will understand each other even more. It didn't take long for Eve to wander off in the garden and was deceived by the devil. Imagine what Eve would have gotten herself into in a 21st Century scenario!

It is also helpful to keep in mind specific criteria that God has put into place as helpful guide in choosing a life partner. What I mean is, there is no single reference or inference in the Scriptures whatsoever that you need to try different relationships before deciding on which individual to marry. This practice and mindset is prevalent and common among single folks in the 21st century. This can lead to confusion in decision making and even result into resenting someone that you might consider no good (not good enough) for you. Pastor Bill Winston humorously puts it succinctly in one of his sermons when he quizzed; *"How many frogs do you have to kiss before you get married?"* Your goal should be to cleave to the partner God leads you to or leads to you. It is common knowledge that those who have engaged in multiple relationships before marriage are at a higher risk of separation and divorce, because they have too many points for comparison.

In summary, you need to allow God to be a major factor in choosing a life partner for you. Don't get desperate or frustrated. It might seem God is not looking soon enough or good enough for you, always remind yourself that God always has your best in mind. Your *"clock may be ticking,"* but always know that God has the big picture (your blissful marriage and home) in mind.

Consider this, wouldn't you want God to be a part of your marital life span? Why leave Him out of about the most crucial part of your life; a time of decision? Marriage is taking a turn at a junction in a person's life. As you pay attention to your affection for the person, sync it with God's standard, it's a sure and safe way to secure a balanced marital life. Wishing you the best!

#2

"The **foundation** for a **good marriage**
is laid long before the **wedding ceremony.**
It is established when two people
begin dating."

TOYIN AKANLE

How Do I Go About Dating and Courting?

This is a very good question. Actually, this is the period you have to be serious about your future, aspirations, dreams and life in general. The dating and courting period is not to be taking lightly and casually. My counsel to you is to regard this period as life determining. Whatever decision you make during this period is critical to a whole lot of things in your life.

Now our dating culture does not biblically prepare young men and women for marriage as it ought to. The modern dating culture does not encourage adequate formation of meaningful relationships that will enable true happiness in marriage. What is prevalent is a series of shallow relational events, which often leads to multiple and successive break ups. At the very least, this culture is as much a preparation for divorce as it is for marriage.

The divorce rate is over 50% in America. Why is this the case? Because people put more value on the excitement and infatuation of the dating experience, than on building a mutually beneficial, godly, long-term relationship.

So, is there anything wrong with dating? Not quite. On the contrary, dating is when two people begin to form a meaningful friendship geared towards knowing and discovering each other. You might say it is the beginning of laying a foundation to build a committed and lasting relationship. The foundation for a good marriage is laid long before the wedding ceremony. It is established when two people begin dating. Marriage should start as friendship. Then the two of you will build the friendship into a relationship which eventually will lead to partnership, that is marriage.

Courtship on the other hand is when both of you decides to take the friendship, dating, to a newer level. This new level involves more commitment and devotion to each other. Courtship period is when both parties begin to put in more emotion, time and resources if you will, in the friendship.

Courtship is more demanding than dating. While dating is focused more on discovering each other mostly based on social events and the likes, courtship requires deeper interests in each other. It is during courtship that the process of growing into each other begin to develop. You might begin to include each other in your plans, schedule and even major decision making.

As I mentioned earlier, the dating and courting periods are very crucial. There are many fine ladies and gentlemen that have engaged in both wrong and regretful dating and courtship simply because they did not see these periods beyond fun, social events and pleasure. It is more than that.

My counsel, as you consider dating and courting, is to engage in godly dating and godly courtship.

Let's start with godly dating. What do I mean by this? What I mean is make biblical standards and expectations the central theme of your friendship, whether you are a male or female. It is a great start when your friendship is based on godly terms and principles.

Though the Bible does not specifically mention the idea of dating, you should apply scriptural principles that guide relationship and encourage moral purity and sensibility. It is a known fact in almost all cultures that dating is a prelude to courtship and marriage, but what many fails to take cognizance of is that the dating period can greatly influence the kind of marriage they will have. The way you conduct yourself while dating is an excellent indicator of the commitment you will have for future relationship and an indicator of the level of happiness you will enjoy during marriage.

The courting period is no different. Simply apply the same biblical principles and expectations when courting. As a matter of fact, biblical principles are of greater importance during courtship. Let these principles be your guide in how you behave towards each other and how it forms the relationship and developing bond between both of you.

I will like to mention here that you should not venture into dating and courtship if you do not intend to get married. As I mentioned in my response to the first question, God has the best in store for you regarding a life partner. Why must you ruin it by engaging in frivolous and carefree relationship that have potentials of causing harm and lasting injuries.

Dating and courtship are for marriage purposes and not for social status or an act of belonging. Don't let pressure of any kind compel you to take a step you will regret and not benefit from. I would rather you learn lessons that will benefit you than lessons that will have damaging effect on you. Most importantly, if you know a friendship i.e. dating won't lead to marriage, it might be a good time to end it and trust God for the best for you. My point is, have this positive mindset that if you enter a courtship, it will lead to marriage. The emotional toll that breaking up causes during courtship is often too much to bear. You don't need that when a bright future is right ahead of you.

Let me share 10 standards you should set for yourself while dating and courting.

- Guard your heart. Do not allow your emotions to run wild.

- Remember you only look as good as the company you keep.

- You are a Christian, make sure you date and court a

Christian.

- Set a boundary for going too far.

- Don't encourage moments that heighten sexual desires.

- Consider the reputation of your potential date.

- Observe if you are attracting the person who is not your type.

- Consider the places you visit on your dates.

- Avoid being alone all the time while dating and courting.

- Take note, if you happen to have gone far, retrace your steps. God is holy and forgiven.

This bring me to another point on dating and courtship; **short term or long term dating and courtship.**

There is no hard and fast rule about short term or long term dating and courtship. The point I am making is that both short term and long term dating and courting could be valuable and worthwhile, or vice visa, depending on individual circumstances and other factors that may be peculiar to your friendship and relationship. What I am particular about is how ready and prepared are you? There may be no need to prolong dating and courtship if you and your intending partner are both ready and prepared for marriage.

Let's look at the pitfalls of both for a second. Short term friendship and relationship maybe based on emotions and not reality. It may not allow the process of growing into each other and developing with each other to mature to a manageable level. Long term dating and courting on the other hand can weigh both parties down. You don't want to rush things and don't want to drag things equally.

If your dating and courting are periods well managed, both of you will be able to discern what is best for you. There are happy marriages that only requires short term periods for both partners to discern they are meant for each other. I dated my husband for a few years and we courted for about four years. To some people this might be too long but it didn't feel like that for us. This is what I mean by it depends on individual circumstances. Don't compare your dating and relationship with others, you are peculiar. Grow in it. Trust in God to discern what time is best for you. Allow mutual consent and comfortability. I think it is much better to marry someone who is ready and prepared to commit and be devoted to you, even if it's a short relationship or a long one.

#3

"**Marriage** transcends just the man
and the woman alone, it involves
the **family** too."

TOYIN AKANLE

Is Parental Consent Important?

I have been asked also how much involvement should parents have while dating and courting. My suggestion is that you should carry your parents along. What you may probably not know is that your parents are as concerned about your future as you are. A good number of people are not aware of the facts that the relationship with the family determines to a great extent the way a person behaves in a romantic relationship. The Bible, having not spelt it out precisely, gives indications that parental consent concerning your partner is very important. Samson was a typical example given, at various times he went ahead to marry women his parent did not and would not consent to (Judges.14:3, 16:1 and 16:4) which eventually lead to his downfall. Abraham also made it clear that he would not have Isaac, his son, take a wife from among the heathen (Genesis.24:1-4, 49-51). God is particular about who we marry and He has also given charge of us to our parent who will in turn give an account to Him how they parented us. (Deuterronomy7:3)

Majority of times a partner tends to treat another better and with more respect when they are aware that the partner's parent consent was sort after or given, the chance of being maltreated is highly reduced. Parental consent also allows for parental blessings and it creates a cordial relationship between all in-laws and family members involved. A lot of people might argue that after all you and not your parents would be living in the marriage, as true as this is what most people fail to understand is that marriage transcends just the man and the woman alone, but it involves the families too. Both spouses' families are also brought together in the union.

Though considered old fashioned, archaic, and domineering by some, believe me it has also accounted for several successful marriages.

Let me share this write up with you. I was thrilled by it. It's from Tulip Gems and it shed more lights on this topic.

> *"And Abraham said unto his eldest servant of his house, that ruled over all that he had, Put, I pray thee, thy hand under my thigh: And I will make thee swear by the LORD, the God of heaven, and the God of the earth, that thou shalt not take a wife unto my son of the daughters of the Canaanites, among whom I dwell: But thou shalt go unto my country, and to my kindred, and take a wife unto my son Isaac."* (Genesis 24:2-4)

Notice that in the passage quoted above, it was the father

(Abraham) and not the son (Isaac) who decided whom Isaac should marry. If anyone objects that this was under the Law of Moses, we reply that this was long before Moses was born.

Isaac received this tradition of parental choice of marriage partner from his father Abraham and passed it on to his own son Jacob.

> *"And Isaac called Jacob, and blessed him, and charged him, and said unto him, Thou shalt not take a wife of the daughters of Canaan."* (Genesis 28:1)

Jacob obeyed his father Isaac and was blessed of God. Jacob's twin brother Esau married Canaanite women and caused his parents grief.

> *"And Esau was forty years old when he took to wife Judith the daughter of Beeri the Hittite, and Bashemath the daughter of Elon the Hittite: Which were a grief of mind unto Isaac and to Rebekah."* (Genesis 26:34-35)

God confirmed this time-honored tradition. several hundred years later, he told Moses to command the men of Israel to forbid their children to intermarry with the Canaanites:

> *"Neither shalt thou make marriages with them; thy daughter thou shalt not give unto his son, nor*

his daughter shalt thou take unto thy son."
(Deuteronomy 7:3)

In all of the Scriptures just quoted above, it is the father's duty to have the final say whom his sons and daughters may or may not marry. And we find the same parental authority assumed in the New Testament. Paul, speaking of the bride's father, writes:

> *"So then he that giveth her in marriage doeth well;*
> *but he that giveth her not in marriage doeth better."*
> (1 Corinthians 7:38)

Our Lord Jesus Christ shows that parental permission was always the accepted way of deciding on a marriage partner—even long before the time of Abraham, when, speaking of the days of Noah, He says: *"For as in the days that were before the flood they were eating and drinking, marrying and giving in marriage, until the day that Noah entered into the ark"* *(Matthew 24:38)*

Why is parental permission to marry necessary? Let us suggest several reasons from Scripture.

- Parents normally want the best for their children (Genesis 24:2-4).

- Parents are older and are more experienced than their children. *"Hearken unto thy father that begat thee, and despise not thy mother when she is old" (Proverbs 23:22)*

■ 23|

- Parents tend to see things in others that their children will often overlook. *"Honor thy father and thy mother" (Exodus20:12)*

- Parents want a continuity of faith and social harmony with their children and grandchildren *(Genesis 26:34-35)*.

- Fathers have a duty to diligently teach their faith to their sons (includes sons in laws) and their sons' sons (grandsons).

  "Only take heed to thyself, and keep thy soul diligently, lest thou forget the things which thine eyes have seen, and lest they depart from thy heart all the days of thy life: but teach them thy sons, and thy sons' sons;" (Deuteronomy 4:9)

- Fathers have a duty to forbid marriage of their children to unbelievers *(Deuteronomy 7:3 and 2 Corinthians 6:14)*.

Marriage is not just between two individuals. It is between two families. Therefore, the prospective bride and groom should definitely seek their parents' permission and blessing before marrying (Exodus 20:12).

On this last point, we may add that sometimes this may not be possible. The parents may be physically dead, or still dead in trespasses and sins. The child seeking permission to marry may be a new convert to Christ. However, even in this situation, the permission of the parents should first be sought. If, however, the parents refuse permission, simply on the new faith of the child, then it is better to obey God than men. Marry in the Lord.

Parental permission to marry is clearly God's Law, but many of us were unaware of it and broke God's Law by not asking our parent's permission to marry. Others may have been aware of God's Law in this vital area, and yet felt it unimportant in an age of grace.

In both cases, however, we were wrong. We need to seek God's forgiveness through our Lord Jesus Christ and then we need to teach the correct way of parental permission to marry to our children and grandchildren.

"Parental Permission to Marry." Tulip Gem by George Thesis" www.tulipgems.com/ParentalPermissiontoMarry.htm

#4

"Sometimes **things** are less about
what we do, than about
our heart."

TOYIN AKANLE

Considering Online Dating; Am I Desperate?

I don't think so. Online dating is a major topic for debate among Christian singles. There are no biblical directives concerning online dating, given that such technology did not exist in biblical times. There are some who believe looking for love online betrays a lack of faith in God's provision of a spouse. In their view, the seemingly endless list of online profiles creates a superficial consumer mentality that undermines the sacrificial nature of Christ-centered love.

The other side counters that online dating is merely a tool God can use to bring two people together; Christian users don't place their faith in the matchmaking site, but in the Lord. And they have their neighbor, sister, or friend that met his/her spouse on Christian online sites and is enjoying a healthy, happy marriage as testimonies.

The arguments on both sides have merit. Like many things, online dating isn't inherently evil or good. Sometimes things are less about what we do, than about our heart. The issue is not so much largely HOW you find your mate, but

WHO you choose as a mate. If you are choosing the man or woman with the most appealing profile picture, or the most poetic ABOUT ME statement, you have a lot more work to do. God has used many formats to communicate, Balak and Balaam (Numbers 22:21-39), the writing on the wall (Daniel 5:5). In the real sense, God cannot be boxed. He can use any means necessary to accomplish His purpose.

Social media is used by so many people for so many reasons and given that most people are connected to one form of technology or the other, it would be odd to suggest that it is a medium God cannot use today. The factors you use in deciding a forever love you met in person must also apply to the person you met online. At some point, you will be together; knowing you choose wisely will save you time and emotion.

Often, the Bible offers general principles over specifics. We can then take these principles and apply them to our everyday lives and the choices we make but that process requires wisdom, discernment, and guidance. So, if online dating is an avenue you find useful to know and discover traits about a person, follow your heart.

Personally, I prefer the traditional face to face meetings in person and that is what I recommend when counselling singles. There are certain vital personality traits that you need to be familiar with that you simply cannot know through social media. Do not consider yourself as desperate if you resort to online dating. There are good godly men and women that are truly ready and prepared for marriage that make use of online dating. Just be careful. Be cautious (This is where I will add that a background check might also appropriate). Be prayerful. Allow the Holy Spirit to be your ultimate counselor and make sure you have a confidant who knows about your engagement online. Take care!

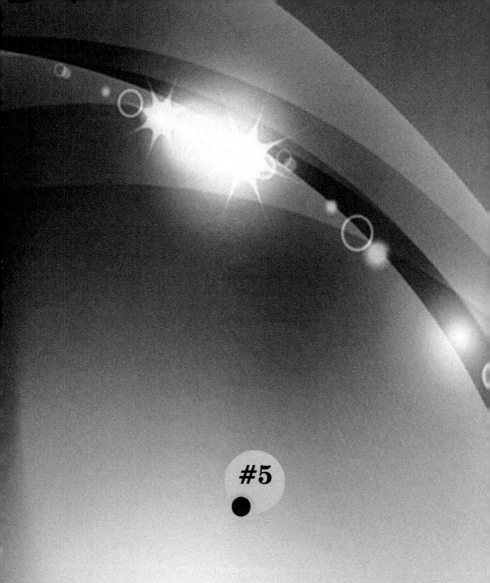

#5

"Whoever finds a **wife**, finds a **good thing,**
and obtains **favor** from the **Lord.**"
Proverbs 18:22

As A Female, Should I Approach? A Male I 'm Interested In

S cripture does not waste time to be clear on this though process; Proverbs 18:22 says, *"Whoever finds a wife finds a good thing, and obtains favor of the LORD."*

This passage does not say, *"Anyone who finds a spouse finds a good thing."* Very specifically, scripture tells us that the wife is the one to be found. This is not the same thing as been cordial with someone and creating a friendship. Manners and interest in people is still important, but it is not the responsibility of the woman to go hunting for her man. Scripture never discuss the flirty, modern, socially forward woman who dares to approach the good-looking guy across the way.

Since the times past, men have been the hunters and gatherers, the pursuers. While it may seem acceptable these days for a woman to approach a man she's interested in, studies have shown that many men don't feel comfortable with a woman approaching them anyway.

Many men find it intimidating or awkward if the woman is

the aggressor because it throws them off their natural "game." From a Christian standpoint, men are assigned the role of leadership. This is true in the church and in the family. This is not a signal of male superiority or to put the greater importance on men. It is simply God's design and assignment of equally valuable roles among spiritually equal beings. Men initiate, women respond.

Biblical support for this position is found, among other passages, in the creation order in Genesis 2, in 1 Corinthians 11: 7-9, and Ephesians 5.

It is the woman's God-given role to respond to an approach from the man. Her response may be positive or negative, it may occur through her father, her family, her pastor or words directly to her potential suitor. Nevertheless, whatever the circumstances, her role is as responder, not initiator. As single men need to learn how to lead, single women also need to learn what it is to let a man assume spiritual leadership in the relationship — and to respond to that leadership. Ultimately, this means learning to trust that God will always lead you to the best and lead the best to you. Most likely the man may misinterpret your intentions. It's simply the reality and the way we humans have been conditioned. There is nothing wrong in initiating friendship with the opposite sex as a female but keep it platonic. Let him make the move in taking it the next level. Let him see your worth and your value and want it too.

It is the woman's God-given role to respond to an approach

from the man. Her response may be positive or negative, it may occur through her father, her family, her pastor or words directly to her potential suitor. Nevertheless, whatever the circumstances, her role is as responder, not initiator. As single men need to learn how to lead, single women also need to learn what it is to let a man assume spiritual leadership in the relationship — and to respond to that leadership. Ultimately, this means learning to trust that God will always lead you to the best and lead the best to you. Most likely the man may misinterpret your intentions. It's simply the reality and the way we humans have been conditioned. There is nothing wrong in initiating friendship with the opposite sex as a female but keep it platonic. Let him make the move in taking it the next level. Let him see your worth and your value and want it too.

#6

"**Christians** outward appearance is a **visible** and silent **testimony** of our Christian **values.**"

TOYIN AKANLE

What Is Wrong With Dressing To Attract The Opposite Sex?

Clothes and appearance are the most powerful non-verbal communicators not only of socio-economic status, but also of moral values. What this mean is, *"you are what you wear."*

Your outward appearance is an important index of your Christian character and modesty is key. The story of Tamar totally gives credence to this; Tamar disguised her appearance such that her father–in–law could not recognize her and mistook her for a prostitute (Genesis 38:13-19).

Our outward appearance is a visible and silent testimony of our Christian values. Some people dress and adorn their bodies with costly clothes and jewelry to please themselves. They want to be admired for their wealth, power, or social status. Some dress in accordance with certain fashions to please others. They want to be accepted by their peers by dressing like them. The Christian, however, dresses to glorify God. Clothes are important for Christians because they serve as a frame to reveal the picture of the One whom the Christian serves.

As a Christian, you cannot say, "*What?! How I dress is no one's concern!*" because how you present yourself reflects on your Lord. Our house, car, personal appearance, and language, all ought to reflect how Christ has transformed us for the better. When Jesus comes into our lives, He does not cover our blemishes with cosmetic powders and pastes, He cleanses us wholly from within. This inner renewal is reflected in the outward appearance.

Modesty is a controversial topic, especially when you add God to the situation. For some, they simply cannot fathom, amidst all the great injustices in the world that God actually cares how we dress ourselves, He does. God cares about everything that concerns us even to the tiniest details. So, in the end, the Word of God should drive our discussions about modesty.

What has God revealed about it?

First and foremost, a biblical definition of modesty must focus on the heart. Modesty is primarily about our motivations. In addition, modest dress is also about discernment, having an awareness of our God, others and our environment.

It is important for all Christians and especially Christians aspiring to settle down into matrimony to understand that what we wear says a lot about us either positively or negatively, it also goes to say that what we adorn ourselves with either gives the right or wrong impressions about us.

The impression we make draws attention to us and if these impressions are negative, we will attract the wrong attention and debar the right one.

Modern Modesty Controversies

In a recent conversation, a woman I spoke with seemed deeply offended when I suggested a woman's manner of dressing could tempt a man to lust. She wasn't denying the claim that men lust after women, but she was emphatic that women are not to blame for a man's lustful thoughts and actions. She's right, of course. A person is never guilty of another person's sin. This woman's protest is, in part, motivated by a desire to fight various rape myths in our culture. No one should be made to account for another person's sin. For every Christian woman however, modesty is of utmost importance, and should be first and foremost on her mind. Provocative dressing is not acceptable in the eyes of God or the church and can also send wrong signals to some people, thereby making the woman the object of attack, in many cases rape.

Modesty According to the Apostle Paul - 1 Timothy 2:8-10

"I desire…that women should adorn themselves in respectable apparel, with modesty and self-control, not with braided hair and gold or pearls or costly attire, but with what is proper for women who profess godliness—with good works." Christian women should concern themselves with modesty because the Bible does. This text is a primary example.

1. Modesty is not anti-class and not anti- sophistication

We should note that Paul is not the anti-accessory Apostle. The force of his statement is positive: "women should adorn themselves." The same word "adorn" is used to speak of a bride beautifying herself for her husband (Revelation 21:2). It is a term that expresses being ornamented, well kempt, and put in order. The question for Paul isn't about whether a woman should ornament her body, but how.

2. Modesty expresses your object of worship

In the context, Paul is talking about how women should prepare themselves for gathering at church. Women are commanded to adorn themselves in a way that is befitting for worship. If they "profess godliness" that is, they desire to show God honor and reverence; their manner of dressing should show that they honor and revere God.

In our day-to-day activities, even when we go to church we ought not to copy what we see in the world. Current fashion trends do not reflect the fear of God. When you go to church, dress in a way that shows you desire to direct the attention on God, not yourself. A person's manner of dress, or even their preoccupation with clothing itself (Matthew 6:28-30), is often indicative of a heart that loves self, more than God.

3. Modesty is about your behavior and attitude in your clothes, not the clothes themselves.

When Paul says that women should wear "respectable apparel," the term "apparel" is probably translated too narrowly: it is a term that encompasses not just clothing, but one's whole demeanor, attitude, and actions.

Ultimately, what should adorn a woman is not just clothing but "good works." As Christians, we are being re-made by God for good works (Ephesians 2:10). Christ died so that we might be zealous for good works (Titus 2:14). Women should seek to dress their lives in works that do good to others, marked with godly love. This means modesty is not simply about what we wear, but how we act, how we communicate, and how we relate to others.

4. Modesty shows sensitivity to an awareness of sin

Paul says a woman's apparel should be worn with "modesty." The King James Version translates this "shamefacedness," which gets more to the heart of the word.

It is talking about a demeanor of reverence, showing respect to oneself and a regard for others. It even carries the connotation of "bashful." Connected to the term "shame," the word implies the idea of grief over sin that is in the world—that a woman would be so sensitive to sin, knowing that sin is offensive to God, that she would never come close to trying to provoke it in others.

A woman would be guilty of lack of shamefacedness, if she presents herself without decency, and deliberately dressing in a way that will evoke a wrong motive from a man. A heart of modesty is motivated by love and respect.

5. Modesty is about freedom, not repression

More often than not, modesty standards are seen as repressive rules that restrict a woman's creativity and freedom. Women who dress or behave modestly are often viewed as dull, sheltered, and unimaginative women who wouldn't make a good enough partner. When modesty is motivated from the heart, the exact opposite is true.

Immodesty is often, a kind of slavery. A woman or a man may be enslaved by his or her desire to attract a partner. An individual might define their worth by their fashion sense, sex appeal, image, weight, or the brand names in their closet. This kind of slavery is widespread because sin impacts us all, and in today's sexually charged, media-saturated culture, many people fall prey to this kind of slavery.

As Christians, we are free from the slavery of sin because we are united to Christ. Paul exhorts us to live out this freedom: "Let not sin therefore reign in your mortal body, to make you obey its passions" (Romans 6:12). When it comes to modesty, we can follow Paul's next statement quite literally: Do not present the members of your body to sin as instruments for unrighteousness, but present your members to God as instruments for righteousness (v.13). Paul wants Christians to have self-mastery in their wardrobe choices, to be totally free from worldly ways of defining worth and beauty.

Modesty is a respectable manner of adorning one's body and carrying oneself, born out of a freedom from a worldly definition of beauty and worth, and motivated by a hatred of sin and a desire to draw attention to God.

When it comes to the subject of appropriate dressing and moral behavior, the first question we should ask ourselves is, "What am I trying to accomplish by what I wear or plan to do?" If anyone I know sew me, would I be compelled to cover up, or behave differently?

#7

"Both **partners** must see one another as **equals** regardless of **Age** and see each other **as one**"

TOYIN AKANLE

Should I Be Concerned About Age Differences?

The Bible rarely gives us age examples. We do know that Abraham was 10 years older than Sarah (Genesis 17:17), but there are no other couples in the Bible where both individuals' ages are given. It is often assumed, for example, that Joseph was significantly older than Mary. However, there is absolutely nothing in the Bible that indicates this.

Age can be important in a marriage, in terms of maturity, but it is far less important than other issues such as salvation, spiritual maturity, compatibility, etc. As people get older, age difference means less and less. Obviously, a 40-year-old marrying a 20-year-old will be questioned, while no one will think twice about an 80-year-old marrying a 60-year-old. The only warning regarding age in marriage is to avoid marrying someone young for lustful purposes, and avoid marrying someone older for financial gain. The best course of action is to pray to God for wisdom concerning any prospective relationship (James 1:5).

If you are a woman, and you decide to marry someone

significantly younger, you must be sure you are committed to making the marriage work, so also a man who decides to marry a woman older than him, must be committed to making the marriage work. Contrary to society's notion that it cannot work, it has worked for many people, and is still working. It all depends on both partners to see one another as equals regardless of the age and to see each other as one. It doesn't matter which of you is older, what matters most is what you make of the union.

#8

"The **man** and his **wife** were
naked and they were not **ashamed.**"
Genesis 2:25

Should I Be Open About My Past With My Intended Before We Tie The Knot ?

I believe that God wants us to be truthful and open to one another. Talking about your past will actually help overcome some of the past pain and could actually make your spouse trust you more. It would be that talking about one's past is not any easy thing to do. There are several questions that comes to mind when such a decision as this needs to be made. Most people believe that the intended party might lose interest and might not want to go ahead, and other people are worried that they would never be trusted again, while others believe that if they eventually get married to the person they have told about their past, it will forever affect their relationship. The book of Genesis 2:25, says,

"The man and his wife were naked and they were not ashamed". They did not have any secrets amongst them, they trusted one another; they were very relaxed and comfortable with one another.

For no reason should anyone hold back information from

an intended before marriage, because you are going to be seen as insincere, the partner would likely feel deceived and fooled. Even if your action is born out of good intention you are going to look bad, thereby bringing problems to the home.

If a man or a woman is God's definite choice for a person, the intended partner would stand with the other because every reasonable person knows that coming clean about a secret takes a lot of courage. We all probably have a past anyway.

Wisdom should however be applied when discussing the past. It is important to tell the whole truth about the situation and not hold important details back. Discussing the past with the intent to hurt the other person, manipulate, or force into silence and submission is wrong and ungodly.

Pray before taking this up with your intended; never take the other for granted. Esther, though the Queen of Ahasuerus, prayed and fasted before appearing before the king, with her request. Esther 4:15-17 (KJV) "*Then Esther bade them return Mordecai this answer, Go, gather together all the Jews that are present in Shushan, and fast ye for me, and neither eat nor drink three days, night or day: I also and my maidens will fast likewise; and so will I go in unto the king, which is not according to the law: and if I perish, I perish. So, Mordecai went his way, and did according to all that Esther had commanded him*".

"1 Now it came to pass on the third day, that Esther put on her royal apparel, and stood in the inner court of the king's house, over against the king's house: and the king sat upon his royal throne in the royal house, over against the gate of the house. 2 And it was so, when the king saw Esther the queen standing in the court, that she obtained favour in his sight: and the king held out to Esther the golden sceptre that was in his hand. So Esther drew near, and touched the top of the scepter. 3 Then said the king unto her, What wilt thou, Queen Esther? and what is thy request? it shall be even given thee to the half of the kingdom. 4 And Esther answered, If it seem good unto the king, let the king and Haman come this day unto the banquet that I have prepared for him. 5 Then the king said, Cause Haman to make haste, that he may do as Esther hath said. So the king and Haman came to the banquet that Esther had prepared. 6 And the king said unto Esther at the banquet of wine, what is thy petition? And it shall be granted thee: and what is thy request? Even to the half of the kingdom it shall be performed. 7 Then answered Esther, and said, My petition and my request is; 8 If I have found favor in the sight of the king, and if it please the king to grant my petition, and to perform my request, let the king and Haman come to the banquet that I shall prepare for them, and I will do tomorrow as the king hath said." Esther 5:1-8 (KJV).

We must also learn to respect and esteem others better than ourselves, recognize that other people also have feelings and can also be hurt. Throwing things to people's faces and not really caring about the outcome has been a major factor in broken engagements. You must also study your intended to know the right time to bring up your past. Also look for an opportunity that might present itself and don't leave it too late before discussing it. Remember that God has made every one of us with a level of ego that needs to be nursed.

#9

"**Cohabiting** before marriage removes much of a man's **motivation** to make the formal **commitment** of marriage within a **reasonable time.**"

TOYIN AKANLE

I Have Questions About Sex and Living Together Before Marriage. ?

- **Can We Try Living Together Before Marriage?**

For the purposes of this section, when I refer to living together,

I am referring to living together in the sense of living as husband and wife, including sexual relations, without being married.

There are numerous scriptures that declare God's prohibition of sexual immorality (Acts 15:20; 1 Corinthians 5:1; 6:13, 18; 10:8; 2 Corinthians 12:21; Galatians 5:19; Ephesians 5:3; Colossians 3:5; 1 Thessalonians 4:3; Jude 7). The Greek word translated "sexual immorality" or "fornication" in these verses is porneia (from which we get the English word pornography), and it means literally "unlawful lust." Since the only form of lawful sexuality is the marriage of one man and one woman (Genesis 2:24; Matthew 19:5), then anything outside of marriage, whether it is adultery, premarital sex or anything else, is biblically unlawful, in other words, sin. Living together before marriage definitely falls into the category of fornication—sexual sin.

Hebrews 13:4 describes the honorable state of marriage: "Marriage should be honored by all, and the marriage bed kept pure, for God will judge the adulterer and all the sexually immoral." This verse draws a clear distinction between that which is pure and honorable—marriage—and that which is sexually immoral—anything outside of marriage. As living together outside of marriage falls into this category, it is definitely sin. Anyone living together outside of lawful marriage invites the displeasure and judgment of God.

Consider these misconceptions about living together:

Misconception #1. Living together first will tell us if we are right for one another.

No, it won't. Marriage is a totally different proposition than simply living together. Marriage is built upon a promise before God to remain faithful to one another. Living together involves no such promise. You could fail at living together with someone you may have succeeded with in marriage. It all depends upon how much both people are relying on God for assistance and love. By the way, the divorce rate of couples who live together first is significantly higher than for those who do not.

If your partner will not commit to you for life, don't deceive yourself into thinking that he or she will be willing to make that commitment at some later point. Marriage is a promise to stay together. Living together for many couples lasts for a matter of months, (some live together for years without ever marrying despite vain promises). Should the relationship hit trouble, it ends and people still have no idea how their partner might have done if they both had taken the plunge and made a lifetime commitment to one another. Now you will never know. You settled for the easy way in and the easy way out. Your shot at true love with that person gets blown away with the wind if you decide to shack up first.

Living together prepares people to find reasons not to get married. Marriage, on the other hand, is based on unconditional love and a lifetime commitment. It is not an "audition" for marriage like you have with cohabitations. All of us are imperfect and bound to slip up at various times during the audition. Talk about conditional "love." It's "I love you" now... and "I will really love you" once you prove you are worthy.

Misconception #2. We are just as committed to each other as a married couple.

No, you're not. Neither of you are "all in." You are both still "kicking the tires." Your commitment is conditional. It's not "for better or worse," it's "for better or else!" the pressure to perform in this case is high; you have been given a free trial by your partner.

Deep down, you know in your heart that marriage is far more than a piece of paper. It is a promise before God to love and cherish your spouse for life. People who only shack up also make a promise, sort of. "I promise to do my best... and to watch you very closely to determine if you are worth it.

Misconception #. Our friendship won't suffer by moving in together.

Your friendship will soon become tense and uncomfortable. You're not married, but you're not really courting either; *"you are friends with benefits."* There is always the fear of being kicked to the curb if you don't measure up. There is no security in this living arrangement and no peace. It is too uncertain, and unnatural. Hence, you end up with a strained relationship that is fraught with angst. Not exactly the ingredients of a healthy friendship.

Reasons couples Ought Not Live Together

One

Men and women have very different ideas about what living together means. Women typically see it as an almost inevitable step toward marriage, while men see it as a no - obligation "test drive." Couples who initiate a live-in relationship under the fog of such contradictory assumptions are already in trouble.

Two

You've heard the old expression, "Why buy the cow when you can get the milk for free?" It seems like an unpleasant phrase, but there is some truth to the message when you apply it to living together unmarried. Living together results in regular, no-strings sex for a man, thus removing the sexual motivation that is part of a marriage proposal. Don't worry about his proposing just to bed you — there are too many sexually available women out there for a man to propose marriage just for sexual relationship, distinguish yourself.

Three

Living together means that a man doesn't have to pursue his intending any longer. And if something is too easily acquired, it just doesn't hold the same value as something that is more challenging to get. I have seen many men who are apathetic about their partner and I have noticed this to be truer with couples who are either cohabiting or who lived together before "sliding" into marriage.

I can't tell you how many times I've heard a man say, "Well, we're not married so it doesn't really matter," or "I just married her because she keeps talking about it," or "I only proposed because everyone expected me to." Their lack of enthusiasm and passion toward their partner is as depressing as it is discouraging and possibly failed marriage waiting to happen.

Four

There is no interest in taking things to the next level. Because cohabiting before marriage removes much of a man's motivation to make the formal commitment of marriage within a reasonable time, living together often causes women to feel frustrated and get stuck in a cycle of hope and disappointment. Christmas comes and she hopes for a ring, only to be disappointed. Her birthday comes and she hopes for a ring, only to be disappointed. Her sister gets married and she hopes for a ring, only to be disappointed. I am sure you get the idea.

Even worse, this cycle often leads to ultimatums — marry me or it's over! — which, in turn, can lead to a reluctant and passionless groom or, just as bad, a woman who tries to fool herself into believing that "marriage is just a piece of paper" so that she doesn't have to break up with a man who calls her bluff.

Five

Couples who live together are less likely to get married. Why? Well, for the reasons I've mentioned that remove the motivation to marry. Cohabiting couples also tend to have a laxer attitude toward commitment and don't work as hard to stay together. When their relationship goes through a rough spot — as all relationships do — it is all too easy to just walk away. The legal and public commitment of marriage motivates couples to work through conflict, strengthen the relationship and stay together.

Six

Living together is not a reliable way to predict long-term compatibility or marital success. In fact, couples who live together before marriage divorces at higher rates. There are other ways to set yourself up for a happy, healthy marriage. Serious, guided godly dating & courtship allows two people to get to know each other as loving friends and determine whether they have a reasonable chance of being a faithful, respectful and cooperative couple with shared values and vision.

Spending time at an intended's house will reveal many personal habits and quirks, while a practical pre-marital class that teaches communication, interpersonal and life skills can give couples the tools they need to help avoid common problems and resolve those conflicts that will invariably arise.

Seven

Very few unmarried couples who have children end up staying together. In other words, a child's chances of living in the same home as his or her biological but non-married parents until he or she is a teenager is negligible. Of those couples that do keep their relationships intact until their children are grown, 93 percent of them are legally married.

This is important, since children who are raised by both biological parents in a low-conflict home are more likely to be emotionally and psychologically healthy than children whose parents are cohabiting or divorced. They are less likely to experience mental health or behavioral problems.

Eight

Living together takes the excitement out of being newlyweds. Being a new bride and moving in with your husband to start a life - and perhaps a family - with those shiny new rings on your fingers to show the world your commitment, is a wonderful experience that many women still desire. Many, couples still live "happily ever after" in marriages and you can, too. You just need to know where you want to go in life, and what choices are most likely to get you there.

Proverbs 5:18 (AMP) "Let your fountain [of human life] be blessed [with the rewards of fidelity], and rejoice in the wife of your youth."

- **Can I Have Sex Before Marriage?**

While there are many documented risks associated with premarital intercourse, research has proven that sex within a marriage has tremendous benefits. One is a decreased likelihood of divorce. For example, a 2010 study based on 2,035 married individuals by the American Psychological Association's Journal of Family Psychology showed couples who wait experience happier marriages, The Globe and Mail reported. *'A statistical analysis of participants showed that couples who wait…enjoy significantly more benefits than those who had sex earlier: relationship stability was rated 22 per cent higher; relationship satisfaction was rated 20 per cent higher; sexual quality of the relationship was rated 15 per cent better and communication was rated 12 per cent better.' A healthy, happy marital relationship produces similar relationships in the lives of children who come from them. In short, happy couples produce happy children."* (Source: www.realtruth.org)

Proverbs 6:32 states, "He who commits adultery [sleeps with another man's wife] has no sense; he who does it destroys himself" (Revised Standard Version).

Colossians 3:5 names fornication as part of human nature along with "impurity, passion, evil desire, and covetousness" (ibid.).

Proverbs 18:22 says, "Whosoever finds a wife finds a good thing…"

In addition to these principles, the Bible reveals the true purpose of sexual activity. After God created man, he was instructed to be fruitful and multiply – he wanted Adam and Eve to be sexually active – (*Genesis. 1:28) in marriage, "Therefore shall a man leave his father and his mother, and shall cleave unto his wife…" (Genesis. 2:24).* God's instruction about sex was clearly related to a husband and wife. He said they would be "one flesh," sexually connected, (vs. 24). "And Adam knew Eve his wife…" (Genesis. 4:1). In King James English, this means they were sexually intimate. Also in 1Corintains.7:5 we are told not to defraud ourselves. (or takeaway pleasure from one another). Also, check out the songs of Solomon.7:1-3, 6. Our God created and encourages sexual intimacy in marriage, but outside marriage it should be considered a sin.

- ## What About Romance?

God is not anti-romance. God provided humankind with His prescription for healthy, bond-forming sex within a loving marriage relationship. It is an essential way for husbands and wives to express love—outgoing, selfless concern for each other. This intimacy acts as a special bonding agent that holds a marriage together.

Only marriage, if properly founded according to God's guidelines, provides the grounds for real love to fully flourish. Following His formula of marriage produces a much more romantic experience and is attached to many blessings.

Notice this biblical reference to the benefits of a marriage relationship and starting a family: *"Two are better than one; because they have a good reward for their labor. For if they fall, the one will lift up his fellow: but woe to him that is alone when he falls; for he has not another to help him up. Again, if two lie together, then they have heat: but how can one be warm alone? And if one prevail against him, two shall withstand him; and a threefold cord is not quickly broken"* (Ecclesiastes 4:9-12).

Yet love—outgoing, selfless concern for others—is not what people naturally have in mind when they think of sex. This is because the key to having such love is only revealed through God's Word.

God, who defines Himself as "love" (I John 4:8, 16),

created sex within marriage. Sexual relations outside of marriage leave God out of the picture—which breaks the link between sex and true love.

While most unmarried couples may "make love," as the phrase goes, it does not mean there is any true love involved. In reality, outside of marriage, a romantic "I love you" really means, "I lust after you." If people call it what it is, it would lose its appeal. Can you picture two teenagers or even unmarried young adults whispering to each other, "I lust after you so much?" How about a famous musician singing, "When I fall in lust, it will be forever?" What would you say, if someone came to you and asked about your lust life? It somehow seems less desirable, doesn't it?

- **The Purpose of Sex**

Sex is a profound and intimate act that holds a place at the pinnacle of the human experience. At the same time, it is widely misunderstood. For its true meaning, one must begin with its Designer—who again defines Himself as "love."

Premarital sex is not God's formula for a successful marriage. It affects individuals, in that it opens the door to lifelong consequences. It also removes the God-ordained training element of temperance and character building from the early relationship. In a couple who waits, each party should ask introspectively, "Am I the person God intends for you?" In addition, premarital sex does not allow a man to develop the determination to be responsible for his role as head of the household and eventually a father who will responsibly teach his children the proper purpose of sex.

- **My intended is asking for oral sex because it is a sin to have real sex before marriage. Is this right?**

Oral sex and anal sex are still real sex acts. Studies shows that both gives degrees of pleasure which should only be experienced in marriage.

When people want to justify a behavior, they redefine terms and find supposed scriptural "loop holes" to avoid condemnation. Most people have at least heard that sex before marriage is sinful, so they state that foreplay (heavy petting) is not really sex. Surveys now show that many teenagers are convinced that oral sex is not really sex, even though the word appears in the phrase. The word "adulterers" in Hebrews 13:4 refers to a person who has broken the marriage bond by engaging in sexual activity, either with a person married to someone else or, being married, with someone who is not his spouse. Think about this for a moment: if you were married or even engaged, and found out your partner was having oral sex with someone else, would you brush it off as nothing important, or would you be angry? Even with all the allowances with sexual behaviors and lifestyles today, I think most people would agree that this sexual act is an act of fornication or adultery as the case may be.

■ 65

The word "fornicators" in Hebrews 13:4 comes from the Greek word pornos. In classic Greek, it referred to a person using the services of a prostitute, but by the time of the New Testament its meaning broadens to refer to anyone engaged in sexual activity outside the realm of marriage.

Thus, Hebrews 13:4 says that sexual acts in marriage is proper but sexual acts between people who are not married as husband and wife are condemned.

What many still don't understand (or don't want to admit) is that oral sex does not decrease the spread of sexually transmitted diseases. Most of these diseases are spread by extended skin-to-skin contact and by the exchange of bodily fluids. Saliva does contain bacteria and viruses. Since the skin in the male and female private parts are very thin and contain numerous blood vessels just below the surface, diseases are easily transmitted whenever these parts come in contact with another person or another person's bodily fluids. Oral sex can be just as dangerous as regular sex as far as disease is concerned. Thus, the warning about adultery in Proverbs includes adultery committed by oral sex, "Whoever commits adultery with a woman lacks understanding; he who does so destroys his own soul. Wounds and dishonor he will get, and his reproach will not be wiped away" (Proverbs 6:22-23).

Under Old Testament law, uncovering a person's nakedness was frequently used as a euphemism for engaging in sexual activity (Leviticus 18:6-19). The laws in Leviticus against incest are described as uncovering a person's nakedness to emphasize that God is not just referring to the real act of intercourse. Oral sex involves exposing the genitals; it most certainly would be an act of uncovering one's nakedness. "Thus says the Lord GOD: "Because your filthiness was poured out and your nakedness uncovered in your harlotry with your lovers..." (Ezekiel 16:36).

• **The matter of lust**

Lust is generally defined as a strong desire, especially a strong desire for something that is sinful.

Oral sex arouses all the passionate desires for sex, but sex with a person to whom you are not married is a sin. To strongly desire (to lust) for the body of a person you are not married is fornication or adultery. "But I say to you that whoever looks at a woman to lust for her has already committed adultery with her in his heart" (Matthew 5:28).

The bible is saying that there is no real difference between lusting to commit a sin and actually doing the act. The results of both are equally sinful. Speaking of the wickedness of false teachers, Peter states, "They are spots and blemishes, carousing in their own deceptions while they feast with you, having eyes full of adultery and that cannot cease from sin, enticing unstable souls"

(II Peter 2:13-14). Oral sex easily matches this description.

"Therefore, God also gave them up to uncleanness, in the

lusts of their hearts, to dishonor their bodies among themselves" (Romans 1:24).

Let me therefore lay the scriptural foundation for this response.

1 Corinthians 7: 2-4; 7-9 "Now concerning the things of which you wrote to me: It is good for a man not to touch a woman. 2 Nevertheless, because of sexual immorality, let each man have his own wife, and let each woman have her own husband. 3 Let the husband render to his wife the affection due her, and likewise also the wife to her husband. 4 The wife does not have authority over her own body, but the husband does. And likewise the husband does not have authority over his own body, but the wife does... 7 For I wish that all men were even as I myself. But each one has his own gift from God, one in this manner and another in that. 8 But I say to the unmarried and to the widows: It is good for them if they remain even as I am; 9 but if they cannot exercise self control, let them marry. For it is better to marry than to burn with passion."

#10

"Anyone who **wants** you to be a **parent** before you are a **spouse** is not God's **best** for you, walk away and **pursue** God's **best**."

TOYIN AKANLE

He wants me to be
pregnant before marriage

I t should stand to reason that a man who desires to have children with you, must also desire to make you his wife. If he is not willing to marry, but willing to lay with you, he is leading you into sin and does not respect you or the things of God.   Children are an amazing blessing, (especially when conceived in Holy matrimony) but also an amazing responsibility.

Many people these days are having children out of wedlock with the justification that the parents love each other, but don't want to be committed to marriage – just in case it doesn't work out. Unfortunately, society has made it easy for people to have as little responsibility in anything as possible. For many, marriage is entered with divorce as the problem solver, and joint custody arrangements become the norm for parents who choose not to marry.   What two consenting adults don't realize at the time, is that their decision not to marry makes the child the unwilling participant in a battle of custody and shared rights between parents.

Anyone who wants you to be a parent before you are a spouse is not God's best for you, walk away and pursue God's best.

There are however people who not out of their doing are separated or divorced, which have made them single parents or become involved in custody battle. Encouragement to these parents is to seek God for matrimonial restoration and help.

#11

"The **privilege** of learning how to be creatively **intimate** with one another is rightful **explored** when a **couple marries.**"

TOYIN AKANLE

How can we be sure we are sexually compatible if we don't try it before Marriage ?

1 Thessalonians 4:3 "For this is the will of God, your sanctification: that you should abstain from sexual immorality;" 1 Corinthians 7:1-3

"It is good for a man not to touch a woman. 2 Nevertheless, because of sexual immorality, let each man have his own wife, and let each woman have her own husband. 3 Let the husband render to his wife the affection due her, and likewise also the wife to her husband..."

Sex is extremely important in a marriage relationship. It brings couples closer together and allows couples to express their love and commitment to one another. However, there are a number of married couples who later on in the relationship can no longer have sex for whatever reason—does that mean they should end the marriage? Certainly not. Sex is not the "Be all and end all" of the marriage. It is important and necessary, but what is even more important is the relationship between the couple.

Let's put another twist on this age-old thought. Make this declaration:

"I am not going to "test drive" anything until I am married; that way we both have 'new' products." On the wedding night, the two of you can now explore the gift and joy of sex. On the other side imagine if you followed the philosophy to test drive before you marry and you have had a lot of "testing" experience then the joy and excitement of your first time with your spouse is not felt. The more sexual partners, the more room for comparison, an increased chance for issues and problems in the future. Let me also advise that if you have had multiple partners, be prepared to have that conversation with your future spouse; he or she will ask about it, and you must be honest or risk more trouble down the line.

From various books and verses in the Bible and as referenced in this book, trying out sex before marriage is an outright disobedience and sin before God Almighty. For that reason, you may never discover the bliss and joyful consummation of sex before marriage, since when engaged-in outside wedlock; it is done secretly and with a lot of shame and guilt afterwards. (if you have currently engage in pre-marital sex or have engaged in it before, I counsel you to stop and ask God for mercy, He is a forgiving and loving father).

Sex is created by God to be good but when engaged-in before marriage it will not help your relationship, and often leads to other issues in the future. When a couple marries, they have the privilege of learning how to be creatively intimate with one another. It is a learning process, so if you are awkward for a while, just ask God to help you find your rhythm. According to surveys, men are easily turned on and women are always encouraged to guide the husbands as to how to give them pleasure.

Sex is best when married couples are relationally close. Work out your issues before intimacy. Talk about what has caused you anger, offense, distance... Good and healthy relationships, equal good sex.

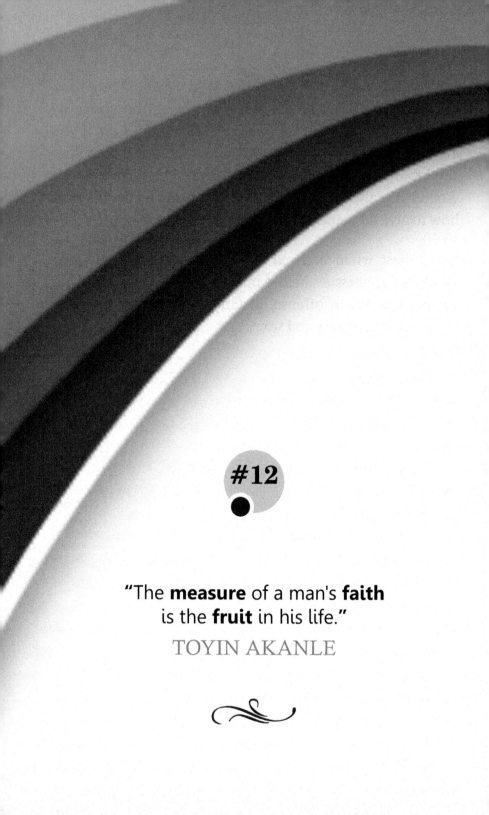

#12

"The **measure** of a man's **faith**
is the **fruit** in his life."

TOYIN AKANLE

He/She is Going to Church Because Of Me. Is This Genuine?

No one knows another person's heart, and everyone is at different stages of maturity and growth in Christ. Some people we know may seem as if they have it together but are struggling with surrendering all things to God. Others may have been strong in faith for years, but backslid. The only way to know what someone is thinking is to ask and be sensitive to details.

- Is he or she in a genuine relationship with Christ?

- Is she convinced that the church is a necessary part of a faithful Christian life?

- If you were not in their life, would they still go to church?

- Is he willing to pray and ask God to give him a love for the church?

The answers will give you what you need to know to make a wise decision. What does the rest of his or her lifestyle tell you? If he is very religious in church but lives like the devil the rest of the week, he's not genuine. He's there possibly for a personal relationship with you, not God.

James 2:19 "You believe that there is one God. You do well. Even the demons believe—and tremble!"

2 Corinthians 6:14NKJV

The measure of a man's faith is the fruit in his life. Scripture says we are known by our fruit **(Matthew 7:15-20)**. The Bible tells us what that fruit looks like **(Galatians 5:22-23)**. It's not enough to say someone is loving, especially if you define loving the way the world does. We have to look to Scripture to see what love is

(1 Corinthians 13), and even more, to what love does.

> *1John 2:4-6 says, "Whoever says 'I know him' but does not keep his commandments is a liar, and the truth is not in him, but whoever keeps his word, in him truly the love of God is perfected. By this we may know that we are in him: whoever says he abides in him ought to walk in the same way in which he walked."*

The most important thing for your own life is to give Christ preeminence (priority) in all things. (Colossians 1:15-18). When Christ is preeminent in someone's life, the things that matter to Jesus, matters to him – going to church for salvation not for show. The church mattered to Christ. A person who is half-hearted about the church is half-hearted about Christ. We can't claim to love Christ and be apathetic about his church. If the person you chose to date feels they can take or leave church, you risk losing Christ. Make it clear that one of your compatibility requirements is shared faith. If he truly loves you, he'll take your dedication more seriously. If he doesn't let him know that there isn't a future between the two of you beyond friendship.

It is from God's word that we are not to marry an unbeliever.

2 Corinthians 6:14 NKJV – "Do not be unequally yoked together with unbelievers. For what fellowship has righteousness with lawlessness? And what communion has light with darkness?"

If it is your desire to be married, it is important that you not linger in a relationship that does not include a genuine relationship with God. Let God lead you to the right person, rightly prepared for you.

#13

"**Verbal abuse** is often used as a tool of manipulation and is usually **effective** because it **destroys** the other person's esteem and ability to defend their own **dignity.**"

TOYIN AKANLE

What Should I Do in The Case of Verbal or And Physical Abuse? Should I Still Go Ahead?

My answer to the question this is No. You are not married to the person yet, and you are abused? You need to walk away from the relationship, before you get hurt, you can also encourage the person to get help. Let it be understood that abuse is an equal opportunity issue in that both men and women are abused in relationships, there is no good or biblical reason to settle for someone who makes you unhappy, or hurts you physically. In fact, this is the best reason to walk away, run if you must.

God hates divorce (Malachi 2:16); it is much harder to get out of a bad marriage than to just walk away from a bad courtship. Even if you are engaged and the abusive partner is not seeking or getting help, please walk away. Many people have been permanently injured, some have lost their lives because of abusive marriages. There are many resources available for both men and women to make the separation healthy and safe. It is important to involve your parents and pastor in the courtship stage of your relationship, you would be able to get the support and counsel you need from them and other professionals if need be.

Verbal abuse is just as destructive as physical abuse, some will say even more so because the wounds are invisible and don't easily disappear. Verbal abuse is often used as a tool of manipulation and is usually effective because it destroys the other person's esteem and ability to defend their own dignity.

It is possible that with much prayer, the Holy Spirit will change the heart of your intended, but why take the risk of years of unhappiness and or losing your life? Marriage ought not to be a struggle from the very beginning. Again, being alone for a while longer is better than a lifetime of pain and suffering, manipulation, and degradation. If you are suffering any kind of abuse, be it verbal or physical; know that this is not what God intends for you. You were created out of love to be loved and cherished, anything less is not your portion.

#14

"God is able to keep you **youthful.**
He is able to **readjust** the timing of your
mind and body to **keep** you for the
appointed time."

TOYIN AKANLE

I Am Desperate, and all the People Coming to Me are Married. What should I Do?

Lamentations 3:25 "The Lord is good to those who wait for Him, to the soul who seeks Him."...

Isaiah 30:18 "Therefore the Lord will wait, that He may be gracious to you; And therefore He will be exalted, that He may have mercy on you. For the Lord is a God of justice; Blessed are all those who wait for Him."

A question many counselors may ask you first is, "Why such an urgency to be married?" Secondly, they are going to ask you, if there are other places you can frequent where there are more   single Christian people than married couples? (for instance, single Christian fellowships or groups.)

Being single is a precarious status when or if all the people around you, friends, family, church members are married. There is the feeling of missing out on something; not having the benefit of a companion, a partner in life. While there are many benefits to marriage, there are also many benefits of singlehood. Marriage is not something anyone should consider in a state of desperation. Marriage requires a lot of work. No one should go through it simply to say they are married. Signing that certificate is only one step in a marriage, not the final step.

If you are desperate to marry because you are lonely, let me tell you, marriage IS NOT a cure for loneliness. Loneliness is a spiritual condition; a condition of the heart that cannot be 'fixed' by human presence alone. Having a life companion can and will fill the void for a time, but it will never fill you completely. If you are desperate for someone to patch all the holes of your heart and your existence, you will always require that of them and you will never be able to function outside of or away from that person.

Work on being a whole person now; wholly satisfied, wholly, grounded in your walk with Christ, wholly focused on your vision and goals for your life. Being single and satisfied will allow God to work in and through you, and he will order your steps in the direction of the person he has been shaping for you.

Marriage is a commitment to sanctification – just like singleness.

How God goes about that sanctification will look different for every couple. You don't know what your marriage will demand from you until you're in it, so don't waste your singleness by living in a state of weakness. Singleness is your time to learn to be strong in the Lord, to learn to live for and depend on Christ. You will need to depend on Christ for more than just a mate. Once you are married, you will need Christ to help you through every growing pain that comes with being a spouse, because you are an imperfect person marrying an imperfect person, no matter how wonderful he or she seemed in Bible study and every function held at the church. Christ is not just for now, while you believe for your perfect mate, Christ is the one companion you will run to more than anyone, and only he can fix a lonely heart.

Marriage will not "fix" you, it will only expose you.

Look at Lamentations again;

Lamentations 3:25 "The Lord is good to those who wait for Him, to the soul who seeks Him."

The goodness of God is prominent in the opening chapters of the Bible. Repeatedly, God pronounced everything which He created "good" *(Genesis 1:4, 10, 18; 1 Timothy 4:4). In chapter 2, God saw that it was "not good" for Adam to be alone, and so He created a wife for him.* Suffice it to say, we all want what is good for us, and what better way to get it than to let God bring it?

> *Isaiah 30:18 "Therefore the Lord will wait, that He may be gracious to you; And therefore He will be exalted, that He may have mercy on you. For the*

Lord is a God of justice; Blessed are all those who wait for Him."

The Lord is going to wait until you too have been made ready for marriage. It is in our best interest to wait on him to create the best scenario for us, to match us with the best fit for us, and to make all things happen for us at the best time. Waiting means you will have the best connection with your partner, the best conversations, the best walk together toward your goals, and yes, the best emotional and physical intimacy.

It is the intent of the enemy to keep you desperate, but responding to that will only cause you to miss the goodness of God for your life. There is no rush to get married. If you are thinking that you will be too old to start a family, something that has been a desire for ages, God is able to keep you youthful. He is able to re-adjust the timing of your mind and body to keep you for the appointed time to be a parent, regardless of your age. There are several stories of women beyond what others consider "prime child-bearing years," conceiving and carrying babies to full term, birthing healthy babies. God is not going to change his mind about you. If it is the desire of marriage and family that he gave you, continue to trust him, worship, and praise him while you wait; focus on being your best for him. Never consider becoming a married man's second wife or mistress, it is not God will for you. You are too precious to Him.

WHILE YOU ARE WAITING, DO THESE 5 THINGS:

1. Enjoy Your Life!

Sometimes, it is easy to think, "When I finally get married, everything is going to be great!" Marriage can be wonderful, but also comes with its own challenges. Resist the temptation to let your thoughts be so consumed with marriage that you forget that you have a life to live. Make the most of it. Travel if you desire to do so, take up that hobby, write the book. Marriage doesn't guarantee any time to do those things. Tomorrow is not promised to any of us so, if you are waiting to get married to have fun, you may be waiting longer than you want. Life will pass you by if you don't embrace it.

2. Keep Learning

Look around you. All the married couples that you see have something to teach you. Either they will teach what to do, or what not to do. Ask them what has worked for them; find out what has helped them create a solid bond. "3. Older women likewise are to be reverent in their behavior, not malicious gossips nor enslaved to much wine, teaching what is good, 4. so that they may encourage the young women to love their husbands, to love their children, 5. to be sensible, pure, workers at home, kind, being subject to their own husbands, so that the word of God will not be dishonored. ... (Titus.2:3-5)

Even your past relationships can teach you something.

Don't condemn yourself for what did not go well, learn from those experiences. No one does relationships perfectly, so even those who seem to have no struggles, do have struggles and issues too.

Take advantage of the opportunities before you; you never know when you'll be introduced to people who also share in your learning journey.

3. Become the spouse you want to be.

It is important to be willing to evaluate your personal strengths and weaknesses, and take active steps towards addressing your weaknesses. Use your time as a waiting single to improve some areas of your life, like improving areas of your attitude or character, practicing your communication and listening skills, overcoming a habit or weak area in your life that you want or need to change (ask your friends, good friends will gladly expose these areas of improvement). Work at improving every day, not just until you are married, but forever. We are constantly changing; minds change, interests change, therefore we must be constantly adjusting to those changes. If you think you are perfect and don't need to improve, where you are is where you will remain.

4. Deal with the issue of loneliness

Everything we see seems to be directed toward couples whether it is the perfect vacation spot, or the perfect perfume to attract that special person, or the meal that will impress your date. Loneliness is part of living, but it doesn't have to consume or overwhelm us. It is important to find constructive things to do when you feel lonely and when you feel like you are the only one out there in the world waiting to be married.

Volunteer at the local library, be involved in acts of kindness, read to the elderly, find ways to make someone smile. You are probably not the only one out there who feels overlooked. Being uncoupled is not a sickness so don't let others look down on you. You are in the best place right now, to live in full devotion to the one who can bring you every good thing; God.

Ask the Lord to reveal to you the places you can direct your attention and energy.

5. Hold on to Your Optimism

Believe it can still happen for you. As long as God is still on the throne, there is hope, and no matter what you are thinking or feeling right now, hope is still in front of you, and grace still surrounds you.

> *"11. For the LORD God is a sun and shield; The LORD gives grace and glory; No good thing does He withhold from those who walk uprightly. 12. O LORD of hosts, How blessed is the man who trusts in You!"* (Psalms.84:11-12)

You are not alone. You are not the only single person in the world. If you believe you are a dying breed, everything you see and hear will confirm that for you, and finding a mate will become an impossibility. If your outlook on life suggests that you know there is someone out there for you, and you will be connected at the right time, that alone will affect how you perceive things. If you trust in God and focus on walking with him, whatever the outcome of your waiting, you will be blessed with his goodness.

"31 Yet those who wait for the Lord will gain new strength; They will mount up wings like eagle......". (Isaiah 40:31)

#15

"A man who would **marry well**
will choose his **life's mate** based on her
character, not on the basis of her **looks.**"

TOYIN AKANLE

Never Settle

In our present society, people give more thought to lots of insignificant things than to choosing their relationship, people jump into a relationship with the first person who shows interest. They commit to being exclusive before they have even gotten a chance to really know each other. Unfortunately, those relationships are based on superficial factors, - looks, financial status, notoriety, etc.

In the Book of Genesis there is an interesting contrast between the selection of Rebekah as Isaac's wife (chap. 24) and Jacob's choice of Rachel, rather than Leah (chap. 29). Abraham sent his oldest and most trusted servant to select a wife for Isaac, within the guidelines he laid down (24:2-4).

The test which the servant wisely devised (24:13-14) was one which revealed the character of the young woman--she would be a servant at heart, willing to give water to the stranger and his camels.

Jacob, on the other hand, chose a wife for himself. He was

unwilling to marry Leah, the older daughter, even though that was the accepted custom in those days (29:26). Jacob favored Rachel over Leah, not because of her character, but because of her looks and her personality (29:17). Later developments seem to establish the fact that Leah was God's preference while Rachel was Jacob's.

What Genesis teaches us in practice, Proverbs teaches us in principle--a man who would marry well will choose his life's mate based on her character, not based on her looks or her personality.

"Charm is deceitful and beauty is vain, But a woman who fears the Lord, she shall be praised" (31:30).

THE RIGHT PARTNER:

- Will encourage you to be your best in Christ, to live a well pleasing live to God.

- Is a good friend. *Iron sharpens iron, so one man sharpens another (Proverbs 27:17).*

- Will have similar visions and goals for the marriage and will support one another in achieving them.

- Will be Mature. An ideal partner is thus willing to reflect on his or her history and is interested in understanding how old events inform current behaviors.

- Will bring honesty and integrity into the relationship. Honesty builds trust; The ideal partner strives to live a life of integrity so that there are no discrepancies between words and actions.

- Brings respect and independence. Ideal partners value each other's interests separate from their own.

- Brings honor. It ought to be the goal of both partners to bring only good and not evil onto the relationship.

So, if the difference between a right partner and a wrong one is so obvious, why do people settle for unfulfilling relationships?

The unhealthy, unrealistic pressure to settle:

Much of society places unfair expectations on others to settle into a relationship. It is important to understand that YOU and not the "concerned" are the one who will live in the relationship. Settling is a major factor why the divorce rate is so high around the world. With Godly direction, being affectionately selective is how you learn to be a better partner.

We are individuals with our own values, needs, and expectations. Just because you like someone, doesn't mean you're compatible with them. Using wisdom is also a major factor in learning to be a better partner, and is how you create healthy, lasting relationships.

Though it doesn't always happen right away, 'Settling' causes resentment, unhappiness, and regret. Delaying the break-up by months or even years will only result in more pain and suffering – and you'll wish you had waited for God's best in the first place.

Why we settle

Guilt. You don't want to hurt a partner feelings by breaking things off. You're not that attracted to him or to her but like the person's personality. Or you know she's not "the one" but you've already invested so much time in each other. So you stay in the relationship even though you know she's not a good long-term match.

Physical attraction. You stay with a girl you find extremely attractive because she's the most appealing you think you can get. You ignore your lacking emotional connection.

Jealousy and control. You can't stand the thought of him with someone else and must keep him to yourself.

Fear of being alone. You're afraid that you might never get anyone like him. You don't want to be alone. You're terrified of having to go through the whole dating process again.

Pressure from family and friends. Your friends constantly ask you for relationship updates.

The ticking clock. You want to get married and have a child and feel like time is running out. You feel your value in the dating scene is decreasing.

Societal pressure. Media, movies, music, and tradition tell you that being desired by men is what makes you valuable. Therefore, if you're single, you must be unattractive and less worthy of love; very untrue.

Blinded by emotion. You have fun with someone and are

attracted to them. Because of this, you overlook all their negative qualities and red flags that indicates all is not well. You ignore their mistreatment, disrespect, and believe you can "change" them.

Dependence. You believe you need him - whether that's financially, emotionally, or because you have a history together (house, child, etc.). You may even think that without him, you are nothing.

The key to overcoming these points is to start building your self-esteem. Realize your worth. Learn how to meet more people so that you cultivate a mindset of abundance. This way when you're deciding to enter a courtship with someone, you'll know that it's the best decision for you. There are some major viewpoints in life you both need to agree on. Or at least be able to compromise. Having your expectations not met is a certain way to be stuck in an unsatisfying and an unhappy relationship.

You should be with someone who makes every day better, not just palatable. When you find a great match there won't even be a question of "settling."

In the beginning stages of a relationship, it's easy to overlook your partner's imperfections. In your mind that person is the most perfect fit for you and even the little nuances seem like something you can easily deal with, or at the least, tolerate without it becoming an issue. It is not until you are deep in the relationship, or the marriage, or even after the relationship is over that you pinpoint all the things that went horribly wrong at the very beginning but you chose not to look at them as problems that both of you could have talked about or even worked through. All relationships have some areas that both people involved have to work through, but there are times when some issues can easily become a big deal in the present and future of the relationships. These are things to really watch out for, they can easily help you in your decision process.

PART 2

#16

"Marriage is most **suitable**
when you have readily
prepared for it."

TOYIN AKANLE

How Do I Know I Am?
Ready For Marriage?

I will address this question by first identifying what makes different people engage in marriage. As you must have known marriage is delicate and it's not something you simply dabble into without a full conscious consideration of the pros and cons involved. In this sense, being prepared and ready for marriage is important. Irrespective of reasons that have been identified as causes of marital problems including separation and divorce, it all boils down to readiness and preparedness. My counsel is that you really need to do a soul search and ask yourself many pertinent questions whether you are ready and prepared for marriage.

Before I plunge into how you may know when you are ready for marriage, I will play with these two phrases; "prepare and ready". It's good to have a little understanding of these words in the sense that it will help you understand what you are about to engage in. In counselling When I use the term "prepare", I mean bracing yourself for what will come and what you are getting into. Now don't get panicky. I am saying this on the brighter side. What I sincerely mean is brace yourself up for both the thrills and pains that comes with marriage. There are myths about marriage that you have to brace yourself up against. For example, Drs. Les and Leslie Parrot in their book, Saving Your Marriage Before It Starts, identified one of the marriage myths as; *"we expect exactly the same things from marriage"* they further wrote; *"What we anticipate seldom occurs, what we least expect generally happens…"*

(Source: Drs. Les and Leslie Parrot in their book, Saving Your Marriage Before It Starts).

You need to be prepared to also encounter different experiences from what you expect. I call this attitude a pre-defensive attitude. It helps you not to be too shocked in marriage. People enter marriage with great expectations, which in the right thing, but this also tends to lower their guard and heighten their anticipation. Marriages started and built on Christ has proven in many cases to be blessed and blissful, but most definitely also, marriage forces might hurl the unpleasant things capable of hurting and upsetting you, straight at your marriage, but at least getting prepared for it will give a clear mind on how to deal with the onslaught.

As for being "ready," what I imply is having the urge to be

a married person. It is the intrinsic and inherent nudge that you are somehow now ripe to be a wife, a husband, a mother, a father, a partner, a cook, a gardener, and whatever role a partner plays in the marriage. It is that inner grace and factor that God has placed and put in you. I will discuss this further when looking at salient points that may indicate you are ready for marriage.

How can you know you are prepared and ready for marriage?

I will like to approach this in a question format. This is because trying to know whether you are ready is better understood by you. Questions to ponder in your mind may include:

· Am I old enough to get into marriage?

· Am I stable enough for marriage? No one goes to war without an adequate assessment of resources. Jesus gave a very good principle that you can apply to marriage. ?

· Am I secure, strong and suited for marriage.

Question A: Certainly, age is a factor to consider in determining whether you are ready and prepared for marriage. Naturally, as a person ages, he or she transits into readiness and preparedness for the next stage in life, which often includes marriage. As a rule, I will rather you look at age (in terms of chronological factor) as something to be considered personally. I will like to use the case of my - mother-in law and 1 as a typical example. My mother- in-law got married at age 23 in 1962. In her time, and probably since she was the first born and first girl of her family, marrying at her age was quite appropriate. Besides she was already a professional nurse then. Fast forwarding to 1993, here I am getting married at age 28. Now in my own time, I still had a lot on my mind to accomplish. What I am getting at is, when I was 23 years of age, my immediate concern was not marriage, not because I was not aware of the chronological ticking clock but because the dictates and demands of the society in my time has altered expectations and aspirations greatly.

So, at what point will age come in when considering life partner? Like I said earlier on, it depends on the individual. Do you have a plan and goal you would like to achieve that is age based? I ask this question because we have seen good folks that had to put goals, ambition and desire aside to accommodate marriage only for the yearning for the old and dumped interest to stir up afresh creating problems in the marriage. This is where the idea of readiness and preparedness comes in. My sincere counsel is, look inward before you allow age to be a determining factor in deciding when you are okay for marriage.

There are others who wish they would rather marry at an early age with a view of a better and restful retirement in mind. Such fellows would like to be done with child bearing and rearing by middle age. This notion is quite ideal in my opinion. My husband and I started having kids a bit late, 36 and 33 years old respectively (not by our design though). From our experience, we would have loved to start having children immediately we got married six years earlier. There are folks who started having kids at late forties and some even into the early fifties.

What I am pointing out is that ideally, it's good to start early, if procreation is to be considered as a factor. Think of what you want for yourself. If you do not mind staying a bit before having children and wouldn't mind to raise children after your prime years, it's perfectly okay. There is no hard and fast rule regarding the appropriate age for marriage. It was suitable for my mom-in-law at 23 and most suitable for me at 28. What's good for you is probably the best thing to do.

Having said that, I wouldn't want you to confuse chronological age with real maturity. This is because advancing in years is a not an indicator of maturity. And trust me, you need lots of maturity to contract, sustain and enjoy marriage. Not even the physical bodily development can pass for maturity. There are many folks of the so called "marriageable age" that are simply immature for marriage.

Question B: To be stable infers that a person need be steady and still before engaging in marriage. I will approach this issue from the scriptural standpoint of Exodus 14: 14. God told Moses and the scared people of Israel to be "…still and see the salvation of the Lord". How does this apply to marriage matter? Everyone needing to be married needs to be of a stable emotion and a still composure. Moses and Israel were stricken by fear and anxiety and the outcome was the wrong choice of direction; they wanted to give up and head back to Egypt and bondage.

As you consider marriage, don't let fear, anxiety, or excitement be the only deciding factor in your choice of a marriage partner. There are many good and decent individuals who have chosen the wrong spouse just because they were terrified of getting into a marriage similar to their unfortunate aunt or someone they know who got married at 49 years old. I have come across several fine individuals who made their choices based on one emotional element or the other only to want out soon. Try and avoid this as much as possible.

Does that mean feeling excited about someone is a warning sign that you might be taking a wrong step or making the wrong choice? No. What I mean is, don't allow emotional elements to be the initial consideration or the only one when deciding on your life partner. Always keep in mind that the element you like, and may not like in a person now, is what you may have to live with for a long time.

It's not only emotional stability or stillness that you will require. There are other things that contribute to stability. Such things as finance, occupation, education, health and general wellbeing are factors that come into play. Now this may seem far-fetched but a good many decent people have overlooked this only for it to pop up during the marriage and puts a wedge in the whole thing.

Take for instance a young lady who decided to get married to a man she feels is right for her. Everyone loved him and few people disapprove of him. It was after getting married that she discovered that the young man has a legal issue that suddenly became complicated and requires a lot of resources to resolve. It did not lead to separation but it created an unwanted tension right at the very beginning of the relationship.

One might want to blame the young man for not disclosing the legal case during the courtship but he did not see it as a big issue then. In such situations, it will take a matured stable mind to accept what just hit the marriage. Many such "surprises" will likely spring up during the course of a marriage and it needs a stable emotion and mindset.

In other words, you should be able to tell yourself to get ready and be prepared to discover new things about your partner and be hit with other things you do not bargain for or really thought about, and living with it. As a matter of fact, a stable mind and a stable disposition will help you in turning mess into an asset, especially if you own it jointly.

Question C: Am I secure, strong and suited for marriage?

I decided to include this question for two reasons. First, you need to realize that both you and your spouse will make mistakes and errors during the lifetime of your relationship.

It will take a lot of sense of security, strong resolve and suitable response to deal with these mistakes and errors; both intended and accidental. Many marriages have gone sour because of unplanned and unavoidable flaws incidents by both partners. Due to differences in orientation, background, expectations and personal convictions some partners are simply not ready nor are they prepared to live through their spouses' flaws and weaknesses. This builds tension and increases negative vibes and signals in the relationship. These stages are not uncommon characteristics of marriages, they can however be resolved if both parties are willing.

It takes a secure, strong, and suitable personality to acknowledge and accept one another's flaws. If a partner commits an error, say of a particular judgment, it should not be the basis to conclude the partner's character or attitude. A ready and prepared mind will know that a marriage package includes living with, acknowledging, accepting, and striving to help amend each other's flaws. Sure, it could irritate, annoy, or completely stun you, but you should always keep in mind that marriage is a long haul full of surprises.

My second reason for this question is that you must also be ready for external challenges.

What was discussed earlier on is internal in nature. There are other experiences that the marriage relationships may be exposed to that either partners may not see coming, or think could happen to them. Take for instance, there is usually one or two persons that will have a strong influence in the family. It could be with one of the partners or both. In such instances, you should not allow the third party's influence to create a heavy burden on the relationship. Both partners must realize that the responsibility of protecting, nourishing and nurturing the relationship lies with both of them. If for example, an in-law, another relation or even friend has no choice but to come and live with the couple, it's best to discuss the issue beforehand. So that the other party (your spouse to be) will not be taken by surprise. Though sometimes it's easier said than practicable, but it's a better option to consider beforehand. In the course of the ministry, I have seen many good and promising marriages ruined and turn sour simply because external influence cannot be handled properly.

Both couples must work corporately to ensure that the impact of external influence does not change the dynamics and tempo of the relationship. You need to realize that when anyone comes into your home, they too survey the ground and it is the atmosphere they meet that they will build upon. When both partners tackle the effect of third party influence, it helps creates the necessary security, strength and assurance needed to keep oiling the marriage.

As you plan to go into marriage, you need to consider this question within you. It might even be a better and profitable idea if you both discuss it during courting. There is nothing that cements a marriage better than to know you will be safe within the walls of that relationship. Strengthen your mind by fashioning out a personal strategy you will adopt should in case a wrong external influence rears its head. Whatever you do make sure you team up with your partner.

Marriage requires a strong and secure mindset with the right mentality to keep it desirable. You cannot afford to go into it weak, feeble, and frail. Get strong for yourself and for your partner. There is no one your partner will need most in marriage than you. You are the best ally he or she would have. It is better to make this obvious right from the onset, and it is by expressing your security and assurance visibly.

Marriage is a gigantic step in a relationship. It signifies the commitment and love you have for someone you want to spend the rest of your life with. While having the strong feelings of love towards someone is essential to getting married, other factors some of which have been dealt with in this book are important to consider before walking down the aisle.

17

Is pre-marriage counselling important?

I will say very much so. Once both intended partners are sure they are meant for each other and are seriously considering setting a date, it would be appropriate to set up a pre-marriage counselling with your pastor or professional pre-marriage counsellor. This is because:

- It practically prepares you for marriage.

- A good pre- marriage counselling addresses a lot of things that you will encounter in the marriage. It might touch on things that you have not even thought about, yet are important.

- It will also help answer some questions you have.

- Pre-marriage counselling especially with your pastor, spiritual leader or professional pre-marriage counsellor will guide you to how to live together in harmony as husband and wife when you tie the knot.